The Poetry Of Emily Pauline Johnson

Volume 1 – As Red Men Die & Other Poems

Emily Pauline Johnson was born in Chiefswood, on the Six Nations Indian Reserve near Brantford Ontario in 1856, the youngest of four children.

Her mother was English and her father a Mohawk chief who brought them up to respect both the English and Mohawk cultures. However times were different then. By British Law the children were legally Mohawk and therefore wards of the British Court. The Mohawks saw them excluded from certain aspects of their culture as their mother was English.

A sickly child, her education was mostly at home and informal by her mother and non-Native governesses together with a few years at the small school on the reserve. She read widely from the family's expansive library. She read widely works by the great poets and tales about Native peoples.

At age 14, Johnson went to Brantford Central Collegiate and graduated in 1877.

In the 1880s, she wrote and performed in amateur theatre productions. In 1883 she published her first poem, "My Little Jean," in the New York Gems of Poetry.

In 1885 Charles G.D. Roberts published Johnson's "A Cry from an Indian Wife" in The Week, his Toronto magazine. Roberts and Johnson became lifelong friends. Johnson promoted her identity as a Mohawk, but spent little time with people of the culture.

In 1886 Johnson was commissioned to write a poem to mark the unveiling of a statue of Joseph Brant, the important Mohawk leader during and after the American Revolutionary War. Her "Ode to Brant" was read at the 13th October ceremony before "the largest crowd the little city had ever seen."

During the late 1880s and early 1890's, Johnson continued to build her reputation, regularly publishing in The Globe, The Week, and Saturday Night. Among the praise was "the most interesting poetess now living."

The Young Men's Liberal Association invited Johnson to a Canadian Authors Evening, held 16 January 1892 at the Toronto Art School Gallery. The only woman at the event, she read to an overflow crowd, with many luminaries. She began to recite, not read, as the others had done". She was the only author to be called back for an encore and "scored a personal triumph and saved the evening from disaster."

The success of this performance began the poet's 15-year stage career. Her decision to develop her stage persona, and the popularity it inspired, showed that the audiences she encountered in Canada, England, and the U.S recognized and were entertained by Native peoples in performance.

Her first volume of poetry, The White Wampum, was published in London in 1895 followed by Canadian Born in 1903. The expanded contents of these volumes were published as the collection Flint and Feather in 1912.

After retiring from the stage in August 1909, Johnson moved to Vancouver, British Columbia and continued writing poems, articles and stories. The posthumous Shagganappi (1913) and The Moccasin Maker (1913) are collections of selected stories first published in periodicals.

Emily Pauline Johnson died of breast cancer in Vancouver, British Columbia on 7 March 1913.

Her funeral, then the largest in Vancouver history, was held on what would have been her 52nd birthday.

Her ashes were buried near Siwash Rock in Stanley Park.

Index Of Poems

A Cry From An Indian Wife
My forest brave, my Red-skin love, farewell;
We may not meet to-morrow; who can tell
What mighty ills befall our little band,
Or what you'll suffer from the white man's hand?
Here is your knife! I thought 'twas sheathed for aye.
No roaming bison calls for it to-day;
No hide of prairie cattle will it maim;
The plains are bare, it seeks a nobler game:
'Twill drink the life-blood of a soldier host.
Go; rise and strike, no matter what the cost.
Yet stay. Revolt not at the Union Jack,
Nor raise Thy hand against this stripling pack
Of white-faced warriors, marching West to quell
Our fallen tribe that rises to rebel.
They all are young and beautiful and good;
Curse to the war that drinks their harmless blood.
Curse to the fate that brought them from the East
To be our chiefs to make our nation least
That breathes the air of this vast continent.
Still their new rule and council is well meant.
They but forget we Indians owned the land
From ocean unto ocean; that they stand
Upon a soil that centuries agone
Was our sole kingdom and our right alone.
They never think how they would feel to-day,
If some great nation came from far away,
Wresting their country from their hapless braves,
Giving what they gave us but wars and graves.
Then go and strike for liberty and life,
And bring back honour to your Indian wife.
Your wife? Ah, what of that, who cares for me?
Who pities my poor love and agony?
What white-robed priest prays for your safety here,
As prayer is said for every volunteer
That swells the ranks that Canada sends out?
Who prays for vict'ry for the Indian scout?
Who prays for our poor nation lying low?
None therefore take your tomahawk and go.
My heart may break and burn into its core,

But I am strong to bid you go to war.
Yet stay, my heart is not the only one
That grieves the loss of husband and of son;
Think of the mothers o'er the inland seas;
Think of the pale-faced maiden on her knees;
One pleads her God to guard some sweet-faced child
That marches on toward the North-West wild.
The other prays to shield her love from harm,
To strengthen his young, proud uplifted arm.
Ah, how her white face quivers thus to think,
Your tomahawk his life's best blood will drink.
She never thinks of my wild aching breast,
Nor prays for your dark face and eagle crest
Endangered by a thousand rifle balls,
My heart the target if my warrior falls.
O! coward self I hesitate no more;
Go forth, and win the glories of the war.
Go forth, nor bend to greed of white men's hands,
By right, by birth we Indians own these lands,
Though starved, crushed, plundered, lies our nation low...
Perhaps the white man's God has willed it so

A Prodigal

My heart forgot its God for love of you,
And you forgot me, other loves to learn;
Now through a wilderness of thorn and rue
Back to my God I turn.

And just because my God forgets the past,
And in forgetting does not ask to know
Why I once left His arms for yours, at last
Back to my God I go.

A Toast

There's wine in the cup, Vancouver,
And there's warmth in my heart for you,
While I drink to your health, your youth, and your wealth,
And the things that you yet will do.
In a vintage rare and olden,
With a flavour fine and keen,
Fill the glass to the edge, while I stand up to pledge
My faith to my western queen.

Then here's a Ho! Vancouver, in wine of the bonniest hue,
With a hand on my hip and the cup at my lip,
And a love in my life for you.
For you are a jolly good fellow, with a great, big heart, I know;
So I drink this toast
To the "Queen of the Coast."
Vancouver, here's a Ho!

And here's to the days that are coming,
And here's to the days that are gone,
And here's to your gold and your spirit bold,
And your luck that has held its own;
And here's to your hands so sturdy,
And here's to your hearts so true,
And here's to the speed of the day decreed
That brings me again to you.

Then here's a Ho! Vancouver, in wine of the bonniest hue,
With a hand on my hip and the cup at my lip,
And a love in my life for you.
For you are a jolly good fellow, with a great, big heart, I know;
So I drink this toast
To the "Queen of the Coast."
Vancouver, here's a Ho!

And He Said, Fight On
Time and its ally, Dark Disarmament,
Have compassed me about,
Have massed their armies, and on battle bent
My forces put to rout;
But though I fight alone, and fall, and die,
Talk terms of Peace? Not I.
(Tennyson)

They war upon my fortress, and their guns
Are shattering its walls;
My army plays the cowards' part, and runs,
Pierced by a thousand balls;
They call for my surrender. I reply,
'Give quarter now? Not I.'

They've shot my flag to ribbons, but in rents
It floats above the height;
Their ensign shall not crown my battlements
While I can stand and fight.
I fling defiance at them as I cry,
'Capitulate? Not I.'

As Red Men Die
Captive! Is there a hell to him like this?
A taunt more galling than the Huron's hiss?
He - proud and scornful, he - who laughed at law,
He - scion of the deadly Iroquois,
He - the bloodthirsty, he - the Mohawk chief,
He - who despises pain and sneers at grief,
Here in the hated Huron's vicious clutch,
That even captive he disdains to touch!

Captive! Butnever conquered; Mohawk brave
Stoops not to be to anyman a slave;
Least, to the puny tribe his soul abhors,
The tribe whose wigwams sprinkle Simcoe's shores.
With scowling brow he stands and courage high,
Watching with haughty and defiant eye
His captors, as they council o'er his fate,
Or strive his boldness to intimidate.
Then fling they unto him the choice;

"Wilt thou walk o'er the bed of fire that waits thee now
Walk with uncovered feet upon the coals,
Until thou reach the ghostly Land of Souls,
And, with thy Mohawk death-song please our ear?
Or wilt thou with the women rest thee here?"
His eyes flash like an eagle's, and his hands
Clench at the insult. Like a god he stands.
"Prepare the fire!" he scornfully demands.

He knoweth not that this same jeering band
Will bite the dust, will lick the Mohawk's hand;
Will kneel and cower at the Mohawk's feet;
Will shrink when Mohawk war drums wildly beat.

HIs death will be avenged with hideous hate
By Iroquois, swift to annihilate
His vile detested captors, that now flaunt
Their war clubs in his face with sneer and taunt,
Not thinking, soon that reeeking, red, and raw,
Their scalps will deck the belts of Iroquois.

The path of coals outstretches, white with heat,
A forest fir's length ready for his feet.
Unflinching as a rock he steps along
The burning mass, and sings his wild war song;
Sings, as he sang when once he used to roam
Throughout the forests of his southern home,
Where, down the Genesee, the water roars,
Where gentle Mohawk purls between its shores,
Songs, that of exploit and of prowess tell;
Songs of the Iroquois invincible.

Up the long trail of fire he boasting goes,
Dancing a war dance to defy his foes.
His flesh is scorched, his muscles burn and shrink.
But still he dances to death's awful brink.

The eagle plume that crests his haughty head
Will never droop until his heart be dead.
Slower and slower yet his footsep swings,
Wilder and wilder still his death-song rings,

Fiercer and fiercer thro' the forest bounds
His voice that leaps to Happier Hunting Grounds.
One savage yell

Then loyal to his race,
He bends to death but never to disgrace.

At Half Mast

You didn't know Billy, did you? Well, Bill was one of the boys,
The greatest fellow you ever seen to racket an' raise a noise,
An' sing! say, you never heard singing 'nless you heard Billy sing.
I used to say to him, "Billy, that voice that you've got there'd bring
A mighty sight more bank-notes to tuck away in your vest,
If only you'd go on the concert stage instead of a-ranchin' West."
An' Billy he'd jist go laughin', and say as I didn't know
A robin's whistle in springtime from a barnyard rooster's crow.
But Billy could sing, an' I sometimes think that voice lives anyhow,
That perhaps Bill helps with the music in the place he's gone to now.

The last time that I seen him was the day he rode away;
He was goin' acrost the plain to catch the train for the East next day.
'Twas the only time I ever seen poor Bill that he didn't laugh
Or sing, an' kick up a rumpus an' racket around, and chaff,
For he'd got a letter from his folks that said for to hurry home,
For his mother was dyin' away down East an' she wanted Bill to come.
Say, but the feller took it hard, but he saddled up right away,
An' started across the plains to take the train for the East, next day.
Sometimes I lie awake a-nights jist a-thinkin' of the rest,
For that was the great big blizzard day, when the wind come down from west,
An' the snow piled up like mountains an' we couldn't put foot outside,
But jist set into the shack an' talked of Bill on his lonely ride.
We talked of the laugh he threw us as he went at the break o' day,
An' we talked of the poor old woman dyin' a thousand mile away.

Well, Dan O'Connell an' I went out to search at the end of the week,
Fer all of us fellers thought a lot, a lot that we darsn't speak.
We'd been up the trail about forty mile, an' was talkin' of turnin' back,
But Dan, well, he wouldn't give in, so we kep' right on to the railroad track.
As soon as we sighted them telegraph wires says Dan, "Say, bless my soul!
Ain't that there Bill's red handkerchief tied half way up that pole?"
Yes, sir, there she was, with her ends a-flippin' an' flyin' in the wind,
An' underneath was the envelope of Bill's letter tightly pinned.
"Why, he must a-boarded the train right here," says Dan, but I kinder knew
That underneath them snowdrifts we would find a thing or two;
Fer he'd writ on that there paper, "Been lost fer hours, all hope is past.
You'll find me, boys, where my handkerchief is flyin' at half-mast."

Beyond The Blue

I
Speak of you, sir? You bet he did. Ben Fields was far too sound

To go back on a fellow just because he weren't around.
Why, sir, he thought a lot of you, and only three months back
Says he, "The Squire will some time come a-snuffing out our track
And give us the surprise." And so I got to thinking then
That any day you might drop down on Rove, and me, and Ben.
And now you've come for nothing, for the lad has left us two,
And six long weeks ago, sir, he went up beyond the blue.

Who's Rove? Oh, he's the collie, and the only thing on earth
That I will ever love again. Why, Squire, that dog is worth
More than you ever handled, and that's quite a piece, I know.
Ah, there the beggar is! come here, you scalawag! and show
Your broken leg all bandaged up. Yes, sir, it's pretty sore;
I did it, curse me, and I think I feel the pain far more
Than him, for somehow I just feel as if I'd been untrue
To what my brother said before he went beyond the blue.

You see, the day before he died he says to me, "Say, Ned,
Be sure you take good care of poor old Rover when I'm dead,
And maybe he will cheer your lonesome hours up a bit,
And when he takes to you just see that you're deserving it."
Well, Squire, it wasn't any use. I tried, but couldn't get
The friendship of that collie, for I needed it, you bet.
I might as well have tried to get the moon to help me through,
For Rover's heart had gone with Ben, 'way up beyond the blue.

He never seemed to take to me nor follow me about,
For all I coaxed and petted, for my heart was starving out
For want of some companionship, I thought, if only he
Would lick my hand or come and put his head aside my knee,
Perhaps his touch would scatter something of the gloom away.
But all alone I had to live until there came a day
When, tired of the battle, as you'd have tired too,
I wished to heaven I'd gone with Ben, 'way up beyond the blue.

One morning I took out Ben's gun, and thought I'd hunt all day,
And started through the clearing for the bush that forward lay,
When something made me look around I scarce believed my mind-
But, sure enough, the dog was following right close behind.
A feeling first of joy, and than a sharper, greater one
Of anger came, at knowing 'twas not me, but Ben's old gun,
That Rove was after, well, sir, I just don't mind telling you,
But I forgot that moment Ben was up beyond the blue.

Perhaps it was but jealousy, perhaps it was despair,
But I just struck him with the gun and broke the bone right there;
And then my very throat seemed choked, for he began to whine
With pain God knows how tenderly I took that dog of mine
Up in my arms, and tore my old red necktie into bands
To bind the broken leg, while there he lay and licked my hands;
And though I cursed my soul, it was the brightest day I knew,
Or even cared to live, since Ben went up beyond the blue.

I tell you, Squire, I nursed him just as gently as could be,
And now I'm all the world to him, and he's the world to me.
Look, sir, at that big, noble soul, right in his faithful eyes,
The square, forgiving honesty that deep down in them lies.
Eh, Squire? What's that you say? He's got no soul? I tell you, then,
He's grander and he's better than the mass of what's called men;
And I guess he stands a better chance than many of us do
Of seeing Ben someday again, 'way up beyond the blue.

Brandon

Born on the breast of the prairie, she smiles to her sire, the sun,
Robed in the wealth of her wheat-lands, gift of her mothering soil,
Affluence knocks at her gateways, opulence waits to be won.
Nuggets of gold are her acres, yielding and yellow with spoil,
Dream of the hungry millions, dawn of the food-filled age,
Over the starving tale of want her fingers have turned the page;
Nations will nurse at her storehouse, and God gives her grain for wage.

Brier: Good Friday

Because, dear Christ, your tender, wounded arm
Bends back the brier that edges life's long way,
That no hurt comes to heart, to soul no harm,
I do not feel the thorns so much to-day.
Because I never knew your care to tire,
Your hand to weary guiding me aright,
Because you walk before and crush the brier,
It does not pierce my feet so much to-night.
Because so often you have hearkened to
My selfish prayers, I ask but one thing now,
That these harsh hands of mine add not unto
The crown of thorns upon your bleeding brow.

Christmastide

I may not go to-night to Bethlehem,
Nor follow star-directed ways, nor tread
The paths wherein the shepherds walked, that led
To Christ, and peace, and God's good will to men.

I may not hear the Herald Angel's song
Peal through the Oriental skies, nor see
The wonder of that Heavenly company
Announce the King the world had waited long.

The manger throne I may not kneel before,
Or see how man to God is reconciled,
Through pure St. Mary's purer, holier child;
The human Christ these eyes may not adore.

I may not carry frankincense and myrrh
With adoration to the Holy One;
Nor gold have I to give the Perfect Son,
To be with those wise kings a worshipper.

Not mine the joy that Heaven sent to them,
For ages since Time swung and locked his gates,
But I may kneel without the star still waits
To guide me on to holy Bethlehem.

Easter

Lent gathers up her cloak of sombre shading
In her reluctant hands.
Her beauty heightens, fairest in its fading,
As pensively she stands
Awaiting Easter's benediction falling,
Like silver stars at night,
Before she can obey the summons calling
Her to her upward flight,
Awaiting Easter's wings that she must borrow
Ere she can hope to fly
Those glorious wings that we shall see to-morrow
Against the far, blue sky.
Has not the purple of her vesture's lining
Brought calm and rest to all?
Has her dark robe had naught of golden shining
Been naught but pleasure's pall?
Who knows? Perhaps when to the world returning
In youth's light joyousness,
We'll wear some rarer jewels we found burning
In Lent's black-bordered dress.
So hand in hand with fitful March she lingers
To beg the crowning grace
Of lifting with her pure and holy fingers
The veil from April's face.
Sweet, rosy April, laughing, sighing, waiting
Until the gateway swings,
And she and Lent can kiss between the grating
Of Easter's tissue wings.
Too brief the bliss, the parting comes with sorrow.
Good-bye dear Lent, good-bye!
We'll watch your fading wings outlined to-morrow
Against the far blue sky.

Give Us Barabbas

There was a man-a Jew of kingly blood,
But of the people-poor and lowly born,
Accused of blasphemy of God, He stood
Before the Roman Pilate, while in scorn
The multitude demanded it was fit

That one should suffer for the people, while
Another be released, absolved, acquit,
To live his life out virtuous or vile.

'Whom will ye have-Barabbas or this Jew?'
Pilate made answer to the mob, 'The choice
Is yours; I wash my hands of this, and you,
Do as you will.' With one vast ribald voice
The populace arose and, shrieking, cried,
'Give us Barabbas, we condone his deeds!'
And He of Nazareth was crucified-
Misjudged, condemned, dishonoured for their needs.

And down these nineteen centuries anew
Comes the hoarse-throated, brutalized refrain,
'Give us Barabbas, crucify the Jew!'
Once more a man must bear a nation's stain,-
And that in France, the chivalrous, whose lore
Made her the flower of knightly age gone by.
Now she lies hideous with a leprous sore
No skill can cure-no pardon purify.

And an indignant world, transfixed with hate
Of such disease, cries, as in Herod's time,
Pointing its finger at her festering state,
'Room for the leper, and her leprous crime!'
And France, writhing from years of torment, cries
Out in her anguish, 'Let this Jew endure,
Damned and disgraced, vicarious sacrifice.
The honour of my army is secure.'

And, vampire-like, that army sucks the blood
From out a martyr's veins, and strips his crown
Of honour from him, and his herohood
Flings in the dust, and cuts his manhood down.
Hide from your God, O! ye that did this act!
With lesser crimes the halls of Hell are paved.
Your army's honour may be still intact,
Unstained, unsoiled, unspotted,-but unsaved.

Golden Of The Selkirks

A trail upwinds from Golden;
It leads to a land God only knows,
To the land of eternal frozen snows,
That trail unknown and olden.

And they tell a tale that is strange and wild
Of a lovely and lonely mountain child
That went up the trail from Golden.

A child in the sweet of her womanhood,

Beautiful, tender, grave and good
As the saints in time long olden.

And the days count not, nor the weeks avail;
For the child that went up the mountain trail
Came never again to Golden.

And the watchers wept in the midnight gloom,
Where the canyons yawn and the Selkirks loom,
For the love that they knew of olden.

And April dawned, with its suns aflame,
And the eagles wheeled and the vultures came
And poised o'er the town of Golden.

God of the white eternal peaks,
Guard the dead while the vulture seeks!
God of the days so olden.

For only God in His greatness knows
Where the mountain holly above her grows,
On the trail that leads from Golden.

Joe

A meadow brown; across the yonder edge
A zigzag fence is ambling; here a wedge
Of underbush has cleft its course in twain,
Till where beyond it staggers up again;
The long, grey rails stretch in a broken line
Their ragged length of rough, split forest pine,
And in their zigzag tottering have reeled
In drunken efforts to enclose the field,
Which carries on its breast, September born,
A patch of rustling, yellow, Indian corn.
Beyond its shrivelled tassels, perched upon
The topmost rail, sits Joe, the settler's son,
A little semi-savage boy of nine.
Now dozing in the warmth of Nature's wine,
His face the sun has tampered with, and wrought,
By heated kisses, mischief, and has brought
Some vagrant freckles, while from here and there
A few wild locks of vagabond brown hair
Escape the old straw hat the sun looks through,
And blinks to meet his Irish eyes of blue.
Barefooted, innocent of coat or vest,
His grey checked shirt unbuttoned at his chest,
Both hardy hands within their usual nest—
His breeches pockets — so, he waits to rest
His little fingers, somewhat tired and worn,
That all day long were husking Indian corn.
His drowsy lids snap at some trivial sound,

With lazy yawns he slips towards the ground,
Then with an idle whistle lifts his load
And shambles home along the country road
That stretches on fringed out with stumps and weeds,
And finally unto the backwoods leads,
Where forests wait with giant trunk and bough
The axe of pioneer, the settler's plough.

Lady Lorgnette

I
Lady Lorgnette, of the lifted lash,
The curling lip and the dainty nose,
The shell-like ear where the jewels flash,
The arching brow and the languid pose,
The rare old lace and the subtle scents,
The slender foot and the fingers frail,
I may act till the world grows wild and tense,
But never a flush on your features pale.
The footlights glimmer between us two,
You in the box and I on the boards,
I am only an actor, Madame, to you,
A mimic king 'mid his mimic lords,
For you are the belle of the smartest set,
Lady Lorgnette.

II
Little Babette, with your eyes of jet,
Your midnight hair and your piquant chin,
Your lips whose odours of violet
Drive men to madness and saints to sin,
I see you over the footlights' glare
Down in the pit 'mid the common mob,
Your throat is burning, and brown, and bare,
You lean, and listen, and pulse, and throb;
The viols are dreaming between us two,
And my gilded crown is no make-believe,
I am more than an actor, dear, to you,
For you called me your king but yester eve,
And your heart is my golden coronet,
Little Babette.

Lullaby Of The Iroquois

Little brown baby-bird, lapped in your nest,
Wrapped in your nest,
Strapped in your nest,
Your straight little cradle-board rocks you to rest;
Its hands are your nest;
Its bands are your nest;
It swings from the down-bending branch of the oak;
You watch the camp flame, and the curling grey smoke;

But, oh, for your pretty black eyes sleep is best,
Little brown baby of mine, go to rest.

Little brown baby-bird swinging to sleep,
Winging to sleep,
Singing to sleep,
Your wonder-black eyes that so wide open keep,
Shielding their sleep,
Unyielding to sleep,
The heron is homing, the plover is still,
The night-owl calls from his haunt on the hill,
Afar the fox barks, afar the stars peep,
Little brown baby of mine, go to sleep.

Ojistoh

I am Ojistoh, I am she, the wife
Of him whose name breathes bravery and life
And courage to the tribe that calls him chief.
I am Ojistoh, his white star, and he
Is land, and lake, and sky and soul to me.

Ah! but they hated him, those Huron braves,
Him who had flung their warriors into graves,
Him who had crushed them underneath his heel
Whose arm was iron, and whose heart was steel
To all,save me, Ojistoh, chosen wife
Of my great Mohawk, white star of his life.

Ah! but they hated him, and councilled long
With subtle witchcraft how to work him wrong;
How to avenge their dead, and strike him where
His pride was highest, and his fame most fair.
Their hearts grew weak as women at his name:
They dared no war-path since my Mohawk came
With ashen bow, and flinten arrow-head
To pierce their craven bodies; but their dead
Must be avenged. Avenged? They dared not walk
In day and meet his deadly tomahawk;
They dared not face his fearless scalping knife;
So Niyoh! then they thought of me, his wife.

O! evil, evil face of them they sent
With evil Huron speech: "Would I consent
To take of wealth? be queen of all their tribe?
Have wampum ermine?" Back I flung the bribe
Into their teeth, and said, "While I have life
Know this - Ojistoh is the Mohawk's wife."

Wah! how we struggled! But their arms were strong.
They flung me on their pony's back, with thong
Round ankle, wrist, and shoulder. Then upleapt

The one I hated most: his eye he swept
Over my misery, and sneering said,
"Thus, fair Ojistoh, we avenge our dead."

And we two rode, rode as a sea wind-chased,
I, bound with buckskin to his hated waist,
He, sneering, laughing, jeering, while he lashed
The horse to foam, as on and on we dashed.
Plunging through creek and river, bush and trail,
On, on we galloped like a northern gale.
At last, his distant Huron fires aflame
We saw, and nearer, nearer still we came.

I, bound behind him in the captive's place,
Scarely could see the outline of his face.
I smiled, and laid my cheek against his back:
"Loose thou my hands," I said. "This pace let slack.
Forget we now that thou and I are foes.
I like thee well, and wish to clasp thee close;
I like the courage of thine eye and brow;
I like thee better than my Mohawk now."

He cut the cords; we ceased our maddened haste
I wound my arms about his tawny waist;
My hand crept up the buckskin of his belt;
His knife hilt in my burning palm I felt;
One hand caressed his cheek, the other drew
The weapon softly "I love you, love you,"
I whispered, "love you as my life."
And buried in his back his scalping knife.

Ha! how I rode, rode as a sea wind-chased,
Mad with sudden freedom, mad with haste,
Back to my Mohawk and my home. I lashed
That horse to foam, as on and on I dashed.
Plunging thro' creek and river, bush and trail,
On, on I galloped like a northern gale.
And then my distant Mohawk's fires aflame
I saw, as nearer, nearer still I came,
My hands all wet, stained with a life's red dye,
But pure my soul, pure as those stars on high
"My Mohawk's pure white star, Ojistoh, still am I."

The Archers
I
Stripped to the waist, his copper-coloured skin
Red from the smouldering heat of hate within,
Lean as a wolf in winter, fierce of mood
As all wild things that hunt for foes, or food
War paint adorning breast and thigh and face,

Armed with the ancient weapons of his race,
A slender ashen bow, deer sinew strung,
And flint-tipped arrow each with poisoned tongue,
Thus does the Red man stalk to death his foe,
And sighting him strings silently his bow,
Takes his unerring aim, and straight and true
The arrow cuts in flight the forest through,
A flint which never made for mark and missed,
And finds the heart of his antagonist.
Thus has he warred and won since time began,
Thus does the Indian bring to earth his man.

II
Ungarmented, save for a web that lies
In fleecy folds across his impish eyes,
A tiny archer takes his way intent
On mischief, which is his especial bent.
Across his shoulder lies a quiver, filled
With arrows dipped in honey, thrice distilled
From all the roses brides have ever worn
Since that first wedding out of Eden born.
Beneath a cherub face and dimpled smile
This youthful hunter hides a heart of guile;
His arrows aimed at random fly in quest
Of lodging-place within some blameless breast.
But those he wounds die happily, and so
Blame not young Cupid with his dart and bow:
Thus has he warred and won since time began,
Transporting into Heaven both maid and man.

The Art Of Alma Tadema
There is no song his colours cannot sing,
For all his art breathes melody, and tunes
The fine, keen beauty that his brushes bring
To murmuring marbles and to golden Junes.

The music of those marbles you can hear
In every crevice, where the deep green stains
Have sunken when the grey days of the year
Spilled leisurely their warm, incessant rains

That, lingering, forget to leave the ledge,
But drenched into the seams, amid the hush
Of ages, leaving but the silent pledge
To waken to the wonder of his brush.

And at the Master's touch the marbles leap
To life, the creamy onyx and the skins
Of copper-coloured leopards, and the deep,
Cool basins where the whispering water wins

Reflections from the gold and glowing sun,
And tints from warm, sweet human flesh, for fair
And subtly lithe and beautiful, leans one
A goddess with a wealth of tawny hair.

The Ballad Of Yaada (A Legend Of The Pacific Coast)
There are fires on Lulu Island, and the sky is opalescent
With the pearl and purple tinting from the smouldering of peat.
And the Dream Hills lift their summits in a sweeping, hazy crescent,
With the Capilano canyon at their feet.

There are fires on Lulu Island, and the smoke, uplifting, lingers
In a faded scarf of fragrance as it creeps across the day,
And the Inlet and the Narrows blur beneath its silent fingers,
And the canyon is enfolded in its grey.

But the sun its face is veiling like a cloistered nun at vespers;
As towards the alter candles of the night a censer swings,
And the echo of tradition wakes from slumbering and whispers,
Where the Capilano river sobs and sings.

It was Yaada, lovely Yaada, who first taught the stream its sighing,
For 'twas silent till her coming, and 'twas voiceless as the shore;
But throughout the great forever it will sing the song undying
That the lips of lovers sing for evermore.

He was chief of all the Squamish, and he ruled the coastal waters
And he warred upon her people in the distant Charlotte Isles;
She, a winsome basket weaver, daintiest of Haida daughters,
Made him captive to her singing and her smiles.

Till his hands forgot to havoc and his weapons lost their lusting,
Till his stormy eyes allured her from the land of Totem Poles,
Till she followed where he called her, followed with a woman's trusting,
To the canyon where the Capilano rolls.

And the women of the Haidas plied in vain their magic power,
Wailed for many moons her absence, wailed for many moons their prayer,

The Cattle Thief
They were coming across the prairie, they were
galloping hard and fast;
For the eyes of those desperate riders had sighted
their man at last
Sighted him off to Eastward, where the Cree
encampment lay,
Where the cotton woods fringed the river, miles and
miles away.
Mistake him? Never! Mistake him? the famous
Eagle Chief!

That terror to all the settlers, that desperate Cattle Thief
That monstrous, fearless Indian, who lorded it over the plain,
Who thieved and raided, and scouted, who rode like a hurricane!
But they've tracked him across the prairie; they've followed him hard and fast;
For those desperate English settlers have sighted their man at last.

Up they wheeled to the tepees, all their British blood aflame,
Bent on bullets and bloodshed, bent on bringing down their game;
But they searched in vain for the Cattle Thief: that lion had left his lair,
And they cursed like a troop of demons for the women alone were there.
"The sneaking Indian coward," they hissed; "he hides while yet he can;
He'll come in the night for cattle, but he's scared to face a man."
"Never!" and up from the cotton woods rang the voice of Eagle Chief;
And right out into the open stepped, unarmed, the Cattle Thief.
Was that the game they had coveted? Scarce fifty years had rolled
Over that fleshless, hungry frame, starved to the bone and old;
Over that wrinkled, tawny skin, unfed by the warmth of blood.
Over those hungry, hollow eyes that glared for the sight of food.

He turned, like a hunted lion: "I know not fear," said he;
And the words outleapt from his shrunken lips in the language of the Cree.
"I'll fight you, white-skins, one by one, till I kill you all," he said;
But the threat was scarcely uttered, ere a dozen balls of lead
Whizzed through the air about him like a shower of metal rain,
And the gaunt old Indian Cattle Thief dropped dead on the open plain.
And that band of cursing settlers gave one triumphant yell,
And rushed like a pack of demons on the body that writhed and fell.

"Cut the fiend up into inches, throw his carcass
on the plain;
Let the wolves eat the cursed Indian, he'd have
treated us the same."
A dozen hands responded, a dozen knives gleamed
high,
But the first stroke was arrested by a woman's
strange, wild cry.
And out into the open, with a courage past
belief,
She dashed, and spread her blanket o'er the corpse
of the Cattle Thief;
And the words outleapt from her shrunken lips in
the language of the Cree,
"If you mean to touch that body, you must cut
your way through me."
And that band of cursing settlers dropped
backward one by one,
For they knew that an Indian woman roused, was
a woman to let alone.
And then she raved in a frenzy that they scarcely
understood,
Raved of the wrongs she had suffered since her
earliest babyhood:
"Stand back, stand back, you white-skins, touch
that dead man to your shame;
You have stolen my father's spirit, but his body I
only claim.
You have killed him, but you shall not dare to
touch him now he's dead.
You have cursed, and called him a Cattle Thief,
though you robbed him first of bread
Robbed him and robbed my people, look there, at
that shrunken face,
Starved with a hollow hunger, we owe to you and
your race.
What have you left to us of land, what have you
left of game,
What have you brought but evil, and curses since
you came?
How have you paid us for our game? how paid us
for our land?
By a book, to save our souls from the sins you
brought in your other hand.
Go back with your new religion, we never have
understood
Your robbing an Indian's body, and mocking his
soul with food.
Go back with your new religion, and find if find
you can
The honest man you have ever made from out a
starving man.

You say your cattle are not ours, your meat is not
our meat;
When you pay for the land you live in, we'll pay
for the meat we eat.
Give back our land and our country, give back our
herds of game;
Give back the furs and the forests that were ours
before you came;
Give back the peace and the plenty. Then come
with your new belief,
And blame, if you dare, the hunger that drove him to
be a thief."

The City And The Sea

I

To none the city bends a servile knee;
Purse-proud and scornful, on her heights she stands,
And at her feet the great white moaning sea
Shoulders incessantly the grey-gold sands,
One the Almighty's child since time began,
And one the might of Mammon, born of clods;
For all the city is the work of man,
But all the sea is God's.

II

And she, between the ocean and the town
Lies cursed of one and by the other blest:
Her staring eyes, her long drenched hair, her gown,
Sea-laved and soiled and dank above her breast.
She, image of her God since life began,
She, but the child of Mammon, born of clods,
Her broken body spoiled and spurned of man,
But her sweet soul is God's.

The Happy Hunting Grounds

Into the rose gold westland, its yellow prairies roll,
World of the bison's freedom, home of the Indian's soul.
Roll out, O seas! in sunlight bathed,
Your plains wind-tossed, and grass enswathed.

Farther than vision ranges, farther than eagles fly,
Stretches the land of beauty, arches the perfect sky,
Hemm'd through the purple mists afar
By peaks that gleam like star on star.

Fringing the prairie billows, fretting horizon's line,
Darkly green are slumb'ring wildernesses of pine,
Sleeping until the zephyrs throng
To kiss their silence into song.

Whispers freighted with odour swinging into the air,
Russet needles as censers swing to an altar, where
The angels' songs are less divine
Than duo sung twixt breeze and pine.

Laughing into the forest, dimples a mountain stream,
Pure as the airs above it, soft as a summer dream,
O! Lethean spring thou'rt only found
Within this ideal hunting ground.

Surely the great Hereafter cannot be more than this,
Surely we'll see that country after Time's farewell kiss.
Who would his lovely faith condole?
Who envies not the Red-skin's soul,

Sailing into the cloud land, sailing into the sun,
Into the crimson portals ajar when life is done?
O! dear dead race, my spirit too
Would fain sail westward unto you.

The Idlers
The sun's red pulses beat,
Full prodigal of heat,
Full lavish of its lustre unrepressed;
But we have drifted far
From where his kisses are,
And in this landward-lying shade we let our paddles rest.

The river, deep and still,
The maple-mantled hill,
The little yellow beach whereon we lie,
The puffs of heated breeze,
All sweetly whisper These
Are days that only come in a Canadian July.

So, silently we two
Lounge in our still canoe,
Nor fate, nor fortune matters to us now:
So long as we alone
May call this dream our own,
The breeze may die, the sail may droop, we care not when or how.

Against the thwart, near by,
Inactively you lie,
And all too near my arm your temple bends.
Your indolently crude,
Abandoned attitude,
Is one of ease and art, in which a perfect languor blends.

Your costume, loose and light,
Leaves unconcealed your might
Of muscle, half suspected, half defined;

And falling well aside,
Your vesture opens wide,
Above your splendid sunburnt throat that pulses unconfined.

With easy unreserve,
Across the gunwale's curve,
Your arm superb is lying, brown and bare;
Your hand just touches mine
With import firm and fine,
(I kiss the very wind that blows about your tumbled hair).

Ah! Dear, I am unwise
In echoing your eyes
Whene'er they leave their far-off gaze, and turn
To melt and blur my sight;
For every other light
Is servile to your cloud-grey eyes, wherein cloud shadows burn.

But once the silence breaks,
But once your ardour wakes
To words that humanize this lotus-land;
So perfect and complete
Those burning words and sweet,
So perfect is the single kiss your lips lay on my hand.

The paddles lie disused,
The fitful breeze abused,
Has dropped to slumber, with no after-blow;
And hearts will pay the cost,
For you and I have lost
More than the homeward blowing wind that died an hour ago.

The Indian Corn Planter

He needs must leave the trapping and the chase,
For mating game his arrows ne'er despoil,
And from the hunter's heaven turn his face,
To wring some promise from the dormant soil.

He needs must leave the lodge that wintered him,
The enervating fires, the blanket bed
The women's dulcet voices, for the grim
Realities of labouring for bread.

So goes he forth beneath the planter's moon
With sack of seed that pledges large increase,
His simple pagan faith knows night and noon,
Heat, cold, seedtime and harvest shall not cease.

And yielding to his needs, this honest sod,
Brown as the hand that tills it, moist with rain,

Teeming with ripe fulfilment, true as God,
With fostering richness, mothers every grain.

The King's Consort

I
Love, was it yesternoon, or years agone,
You took in yours my hands,
And placed me close beside you on the throne
Of Oriental lands?

The truant hour came back at dawn to-day,
Across the hemispheres,
And bade my sleeping soul retrace its way
These many hundred years.

And all my wild young life returned, and ceased
The years that lie between,
When you were King of Egypt, and The East,
And I was Egypt's queen.

II
I feel again the lengths of silken gossamer enfold
My body and my limbs in robes of emerald and gold.
I feel the heavy sunshine, and the weight of languid heat
That crowned the day you laid the royal jewels at my feet.

You wound my throat with jacinths, green and glist'ning serpent-wise,
My hot, dark throat that pulsed beneath the ardour of your eyes;
And centuries have failed to cool the memory of your hands
That bound about my arms those massive, pliant golden bands.

You wreathed around my wrists long ropes of coral and of jade,
And beaten gold that clung like coils of kisses love-inlaid;
About my naked ankles tawny topaz chains you wound,
With clasps of carven onyx, ruby-rimmed and golden bound.

But not for me the Royal Pearls to bind about my hair.

The Legend Of Qu'appelle Valley

I am the one who loved her as my life,
Had watched her grow to sweet young womanhood;
Won the dear privilege to call her wife,
And found the world, because of her, was good.
I am the one who heard the spirit voice,
Of which the paleface settlers love to tell;
From whose strange story they have made their choice
Of naming this fair valley the "Qu'Appelle."

She had said fondly in my eager ear
"When Indian summer smiles with dusky lip,

Come to the lakes, I will be first to hear
The welcome music of thy paddle dip.
I will be first to lay in thine my hand,
To whisper words of greeting on the shore;
And when thou would'st return to thine own land,
I'll go with thee, thy wife for evermore."

Not yet a leaf had fallen, not a tone
Of frost upon the plain ere I set forth,
Impatient to possess her as my own
This queen of all the women of the North.
I rested not at even or at dawn,
But journeyed all the dark and daylight through
Until I reached the Lakes, and, hurrying on,
I launched upon their bosom my canoe.

Of sleep or hunger then I took no heed,
But hastened o'er their leagues of waterways;
But my hot heart outstripped my paddle's speed
And waited not for distance or for days,
But flew before me swifter than the blade
Of magic paddle ever cleaved the Lake,
Eager to lay its love before the maid,
And watch the lovelight in her eyes awake.

So the long days went slowly drifting past;
It seemed that half my life must intervene
Before the morrow, when I said at last
"One more day's journey and I win my queen!"
I rested then, and, drifting, dreamed the more
Of all the happiness I was to claim,
When suddenly from out the shadowed shore,
I heard a voice speak tenderly my name.

"Who calls?" I answered; no reply; and long
I stilled my paddle blade and listened. Then
Above the night wind's melancholy song
I heard distinctly that strange voice again
A woman's voice, that through the twilight came
Like to a soul unborn, a song unsung.

I leaned and listened, yes, she spoke my name,
And then I answered in the quaint French tongue,
"Qu'Appelle? Qu'Appelle?" No answer, and the night
Seemed stiller for the sound, till round me fell
The far-off echoes from the far-off height
"Qu'Appelle?" my voice came back, "Qu'Appelle? Qu'Appelle?"
This and no more; I called aloud until
I shuddered as the gloom of night increased,
And, like a pallid spectre wan and chill,
The moon arose in silence in the east.

I dare not linger on the moment when
My boat I beached beside her tepee door;
I heard the wail of women and of men,
I saw the death-fires lighted on the shore.
No language tells the torture or the pain,
The bitterness that flooded all my life,
When I was led to look on her again,
That queen of women pledged to be my wife.
To look upon the beauty of her face,
The still closed eyes, the lips that knew no breath;
To look, to learn, to realize my place
Had been usurped by my one rival - Death.
A storm of wrecking sorrow beat and broke
About my heart, and life shut out its light
Till through my anguish someone gently spoke,
And said, "Twice did she call for thee last night."

I started up and bending o'er my dead,
Asked when did her sweet lips in silence close.
"She called thy name - then passed away," they said,
"Just on the hour whereat the moon arose."

Among the lonely Lakes I go no more,
For she who made their beauty is not there;
The paleface rears his tepee on the shore
And says the vale is fairest of the fair.
Full many years have vanished since, but still
The voyageurs beside the campfire tell
How, when the moonrise tips the distant hill,
They hear strange voices through the silence swell.
The paleface loves the haunted lakes they say,
And journeys far to watch their beauty spread
Before his vision; but to me the day,
The night, the hour, the seasons are all dead.
I listen heartsick, while the hunters tell
Why white men named the valley The Qu'Appelle.

The Mariner
"Wreck and stray and castaway." SWINBURNE.

Once more adrift.
O'er dappling sea and broad lagoon,
O'er frowning cliff and yellow dune,
The long, warm lights of afternoon
Like jewel dustings sift.

Once more awake.
I dreamed an hour of port and quay,
Of anchorage not meant for me;
The sea, the sea, the hungry sea
Came rolling up the break.

Once more afloat.
The billows on my moorings press't,
They drove me from my moment's rest,
And now a portless sea I breast,
And shelterless my boat.

Once more away.
The harbour lights are growing dim,
The shore is but a purple rim,
The sea outstretches grey and grim.
Away, away, away!

Once more at sea,
The old, old sea I used to sail,
The battling tide, the blowing gale,
The waves with ceaseless under-wail
The life that used to be.

The Pilot Of The Plains

``False,' they said, ``thy Pale-face lover, from the land of waking morn ;
Rise and wed thy Redskin wooer, nobler warrior ne'er was born ;
Cease thy watching, cease thy dreaming,
Show the white thine Indian scorn.'
Thus they taunted her, declaring, ``He remembers naught of thee :
Likely some white maid he wooeth, far beyond the inland sea.'
But she answered ever kindly,
``He will come again to me,'
Till the dusk of Indian summer crept athwart the western skies ;
But a deeper dusk was burning in her dark and dreaming eyes,
As she scanned the rolling prairie,
Where the foothills fall, and rise.
Till the autumn came and vanished, till the season of the rains,
Till the western world lay fettered in midwinter's crystal chains,
Still she listened for his coming,
Still she watched the distant plains.
Then a night with nor'land tempest, nor'land snows a-swirling fast,
Out upon the pathless prairie came the Pale-face through the blast,
Calling, calling, ``Yakonwita,
I am coming, love, at last.'
Hovered night above, about him, dark its wings and cold and dread ;
Never unto trail or tepee were his straying footsteps led ;
Till benumbed, he sank, and pillowed
On the drifting snows his head,
Saying, ``O! my Yakonwita call me, call me, be my guide
To the lodge beyond the prairie-for I vowed ere winter died
I would come again, belovèd ;
I would claim my Indian bride.'
``Yakonwita, Yakonwita! ' Oh, the dreariness that strains
Through the voice that calling, quivers, till a whisper but remains,
``Yakonwita, Yakonwita,

I am lost upon the plains.'
But the Silent Spirit hushed him, lulled him as he cried anew,
``Save me, save me! O! beloved, I am Pale but I am true.
Yakonwita, Yakonwita
I am dying, love, for you.'
Leagues afar, across the prairie, she had risen from her bed,
Roused her kinsmen from their slumber : ``He has come to-night,' she said.
``I can hear him calling, calling ;
But his voice is as the dead.
``Listen! ' and they sate all silent, while the tempest louder grew,
And a spirit-voice called faintly, ``I am dying, love, for you.'
Then they wailed, ``O! Yakonwita.
He was Pale, but he was true.'
Wrapped she then her ermine round her, stepped without the tepee door,
Saying, ``I must follow, follow, though he call for evermore,
Yakonwita, Yakonwita ; '
And they never saw her more.
Late at night, say Indian hunters, when the starlight clouds or wanes,
Far away they see a maiden, misty as the autumn rains,
Guiding with her lamp of moonlight
Hunters lost upon the plains.

The Quill Worker
Plains, plains, and the prairie land which the sunlight floods and fills,
To the north the open country, southward the Cyprus Hills;
Never a bit of woodland, never a rill that flows,
Only a stretch of cactus beds, and the wild, sweet prairie rose;
Never a habitation, save where in the far south-west
A solitary tepee lifts its solitary crest,
Where Neykia in the doorway, crouched in the red sunshine,
Broiders her buckskin mantle with the quills of the porcupine.

Neykia, the Sioux chief's daughter, she with the foot that flies,
She with the hair of midnight and the wondrous midnight eyes,
She with the deft brown fingers, she with the soft, slow smile,
She with the voice of velvet and the thoughts that dream the while,
"Whence come the vague to-morrows? Where do the yesters fly?
What is beyond the border of the prairie and the sky?
Does the maid in the Land of Morning sit in the red sunshine,
Broidering her buckskin mantle with the quills of the porcupine?"

So Neykia, in the westland, wonders and works away,
Far from the fret and folly of the "Land of Waking Day."
And many the pale-faced trader who stops at the tepee door
For a smile from the sweet, shy worker, and a sigh when the hour is o'er.
For they know of a young red hunter who oftentimes has stayed
To rest and smoke with her father, tho' his eyes were on the maid;
And the moons will not be many ere she in the red sunshine
Will broider his buckskin mantle with the quills of the porcupine.

The Riders Of The Plains

Who is it lacks the knowledge? Who are the curs that dare
To whine and sneer that they do not fear the whelps in the Lion's lair?
But we of the North will answer, while life in the North remains,
Let the curs beware lest the whelps they dare are the Riders of the Plains;
For these are the kind whose muscle makes the power of the Lion's jaw,
And they keep the peace of our people and the honour of British law.

A woman has painted a picture, 'tis a neat little bit of art
The critics aver, and it roused up for her the love of the big British heart.
'Tis a sketch of an English bulldog that tigers would scarce attack,
And round and about and beneath him is painted the Union Jack.
With its blaze of colour, and courage, its daring in every fold,
And underneath is the title, "What we have we'll hold."
'Tis a picture plain as a mirror, but the reflex it contains
Is the counterpart of the life and heart of the Riders of the Plains;
For like to that flag and that motto, and the power of that bulldog's jaw,
They keep the peace of our people and the honour of British law.

These are the fearless fighters, whose life in the open lies,
Who never fail on the prairie trail 'neath the Territorial skies,
Who have laughed in the face of the bullets and the edge of the rebels' steel,
Who have set their ban on the lawless man with his crime beneath their heel;
These are the men who battle the blizzards, the suns, the rains,
These are the famed that the North has named the "Riders of the Plains,"
And theirs is the might and the meaning and the strength of the bulldog's jaw,
While they keep the peace of the people and the honour of British law.

These are the men of action, who need not the world's renown,
For their valour is known to England's throne as a gem in the British crown;
These are the men who face the front, whose courage the world may scan,
The men who are feared by the felon, but are loved by the honest man;
These are the marrow, the pith, the cream, the best that the blood contains,
Who have cast their days in the valiant ways of the Riders of the Plains;
And theirs is the kind whose muscle makes the power of old England's jaw,
And they keep the peace of her people and the honour of British law.

Then down with the cur that questions, let him slink to his craven den,
For he daren't deny our hot reply as to "who are our mounted men."
He shall honour them east and westward, he shall honour them south and north,
He shall bare his head to that coat of red wherever that red rides forth.
'Tis well that he knows the fibre that the great North-West contains,
The North-West pride in her men that ride on the Territorial plains,
For of such as these are the muscles and the teeth in the Lion's jaw,
And they keep the peace of our people and the honour of British law.

The Songster

Music, music with throb and swing,
Of a plaintive note, and long;
'Tis a note no human throat could sing,

No harp with its dulcet golden string,
Nor lute, nor lyre with liquid ring,
Is sweet as the robin's song.

He sings for love of the season
When the days grow warm and long,
For the beautiful God-sent reason
That his breast was born for song.

Calling, calling so fresh and clear,
Through the song-sweet days of May;
Warbling there, and whistling here,
He swells his voice on the drinking ear,
On the great, wide, pulsing atmosphere
Till his music drowns the day.

He sings for love of the season
When the days grow warm and long,
For the beautiful God-sent reason
That his breast was born for song.

The Trail To Lillooet

Sob of fall, and song of forest, come you here on haunting quest,
Calling through the seas and silence, from God's country of the west.
Where the mountain pass is narrow, and the torrent white and strong,
Down its rocky-throated canyon, sings its golden-throated song.

You are singing there together through the God-begotten nights,
And the leaning stars are listening above the distant heights
That lift like points of opal in the crescent coronet
About whose golden setting sweeps the trail to Lillooet.

Trail that winds and trail that wanders, like a cobweb hanging high,
Just a hazy thread outlining mid-way of the stream and sky,
Where the Fraser River canyon yawns its pathway to the sea,
But half the world has shouldered up between its song and me.

Here, the placid English August, and the sea-encircled miles,
There God's copper-coloured sunshine beating through the lonely aisles
Where the waterfalls and forest voice for ever their duet,
And call across the canyon on the trail to Lillooet.

The Vagabonds

What saw you in your flight to-day,
Crows, awinging your homeward way?

Went you far in carrion quest,
Crows, that worry the sunless west?

Thieves and villains, you shameless things!

Black your record as black your wings.

Tell me, birds of the inky hue,
Plunderous rogues to-day have you

Seen with mischievous, prying eyes
Lands where earlier suns arise?

Saw you a lazy beck between
Trees that shadow its breast in green,

Teased by obstinate stones that lie
Crossing the current tauntingly?

Fields abloom on the farther side
With purpling clover lying wide

Saw you there as you circled by,
Vale-environed a cottage lie,

Girt about with emerald bands,
Nestling down in its meadow lands?

Saw you this on your thieving raids?
Speak you rascally renegades!

Thieved you also away from me
Olden scenes that I long to see?

If, O! crows, you have flown since morn
Over the place where I was born,

Forget will I, how black you were
Since dawn, in feather and character;

Absolve will I, your vagrant band
Ere you enter your slumberland.

Through Time And Bitter Distance
Unknown to you, I walk the cheerless shore.
The cutting blast, the hurl of biting brine
May freeze, and still, and bind the waves at war,
Ere you will ever know, O! Heart of mine,
That I have sought, reflected in the blue
Of these sea depths, some shadow of your eyes;
Have hoped the laughing waves would sing of you,
But this is all my starving sight descries-

I
Far out at sea a sail
Bends to the freshening breeze,

Yields to the rising gale
That sweeps the seas;

II
Yields, as a bird wind-tossed,
To saltish waves that fling
Their spray, whose rime and frost
Like crystals cling

III
To canvas, mast and spar,
Till, gleaming like a gem,
She sinks beyond the far
Horizon's hem.

IV
Lost to my longing sight,
And nothing left to me
Save an oncoming night,-
An empty sea.

Wave-won
To-night I hunger so,
Beloved one, to know
If you recall and crave again the dream
That haunted our canoe,
And wove its witchcraft through
Our hearts as 'neath the northern night we sailed the northern stream.

Ah! dear, if only we
As yesternight could be
Afloat within that light and lonely shell,
To drift in silence till
Heart-hushed, and lulled and still
The moonlight through the melting air flung forth its fatal spell.

The dusky summer night,
The path of gold and white
The moon had cast across the river's breast,
The shores in shadows clad,
The far-away, half-sad
Sweet singing of the whip-poor-will, all soothed our souls to rest.

You trusted I could feel
My arm as strong as steel,
So still your upturned face, so calm your breath,
While circling eddies curled,
While laughing rapids whirled
From boulder unto boulder, till they dashed themselves to death.

Your splendid eyes aflame

Put heaven's stars to shame,
Your god-like head so near my lap was laid
My hand is burning where
It touched your wind-blown hair,
As sweeping to the rapids verge, I changed my paddle blade.

The boat obeyed my hand,
Till wearied with its grand
Wild anger, all the river lay aswoon,
And as my paddle dipped,
Thro' pools of pearl it slipped
And swept beneath a shore of shade, beneath a velvet moon.

To-night, again dream you
Our spirit-winged canoe
Is listening to the rapids purling past?
Where, in delirium reeled
Our maddened hearts that kneeled
To idolize the perfect world, to taste of love at last.

When George Was King

Cards, and swords, and a lady's love,
That is a tale worth reading,
An insult veiled, a downcast glove,
And rapiers leap unheeding.
And 'tis O! for the brawl,
The thrust, the fall,
And the foe at your feet a-bleeding.

Tales of revel at wayside inns,
The goblets gaily filling,
Braggarts boasting a thousand sins,
Though none can boast a shilling.
And 'tis O! for the wine,
The frothing stein,
And the clamour of cups a-spilling.

Tales of maidens in rich brocade,
Powder and puff and patches,
Gallants lilting a serenade
Of old-time trolls and catches.
And 'tis O! for the lips
And the finger tips,
And the kiss that the boldest snatches.

Tales of buckle and big rosette,
The slender shoe adorning,
Of curtseying through the minuet
With laughter, love, or scorning.
And 'tis O! for the shout
Of the roustabout,

As he hies him home in the morning.

Cards and swords, and a lady's love,
Give to the tale God-speeding,
War and wassail, and perfumed glove,
And all that's rare in reading.
And 'tis O! for the ways
Of the olden days,
And a life that was worth the leading.

Where Leaps The Ste. Marie

I
What dream you in the night-time
When you whisper to the moon?
What say you in the morning?
What do you sing at noon?
When I hear your voice uplifting,
Like a breeze through branches sifting,
And your ripples softly drifting
To the August airs a-tune.

II
Lend me your happy laughter,
Ste. Marie, as you leap;
Your peace that follows after
Where through the isles you creep.
Give to me your splendid dashing,
Give your sparkles and your splashing,
Your uphurling waves down crashing,
Then, your aftermath of sleep.

Workworn

Across the street, an humble woman lives;
To her 'tis little fortune ever gives;
Denied the wines of life, it puzzles me
To know how she can laugh so cheerily.
This morn I listened to her softly sing,
And, marvelling what this effect could bring
I looked: 'twas but the presence of a child
Who passed her gate, and looking in, had smiled.
But self-encrusted, I had failed to see
The child had also looked and laughed to me.
My lowly neighbour thought the smile God-sent,
And singing, through the toilsome hours she went.
O! weary singer, I have learned the wrong
Of taking gifts, and giving naught of song;
I thought my blessings scant, my mercies few,
Till I contrasted them with yours, and you;
To-day I counted much, yet wished it more
While but a child's bright smile was all your store,

If I had thought of all the stormy days,
That fill some lives that tread less favoured ways,
How little sunshine through their shadows gleamed,
My own dull life had much the brighter seemed;
If I had thought of all the eyes that weep
Through desolation, and still smiling keep,
That see so little pleasure, so much woe,
My own had laughed more often long ago;
If I had thought how leaden was the weight
Adversity lays at my kinsman's gate,
Of that great cross my next door neighbour bears,
My thanks had been more frequent in my prayers;
If I had watched the woman o'er the way,
Workworn and old, who labours day by day,
Who has no rest, no joy to call her own,
My tasks, my heart, had much the lighter grown.

Your Mirror Frame

Methinks I see your mirror frame,
Ornate with photographs of them.
Place mine therein, for, all the same,
I'll have my little laughs at them.

For girls may come, and girls may go,
I think I have the best of them;
And yet this photograph I know
You'll toss among the rest of them.

I cannot even hope that you
Will put me in your locket, dear;
Nor costly frame will I look through,
Nor bide in your breast pocket, dear.

For none your heart monopolize,
You favour such a nest of them.
So I but hope your roving eyes
Seek mine among the rest of them.

For saucy sprite, and noble dame,
And many a dainty maid of them
Will greet me in your mirror frame,
And share your kisses laid on them.

And yet, sometimes I fancy, dear,
You hold me as the best of them.
So I'm content if I appear
To-night with all the rest of them.

www.ingramcontent.com/pod-product-compliance
Lightning Source LLC
Chambersburg PA
CBHW060104050426
42448CB00011B/2616